# Simple Pleasures for BUSY COUPLES

**DIMENSIONS FOR LIVING**

NASHVILLE

Simple Pleasures for Busy Couples

Copyright ©1997 by Dimensions for Living

All rights reserved.

No part of this work may be reproduced or transmitted in any form or by any means, electronic or mechanical, including photocopying and recording, or by any information service or retrieval system, except as may be expressly permitted by the 1976 Copyright Act or in writing from the publisher. Requests for permission should be addressed to Dimensions for Living, P.O. Box 801, 201 Eighth Avenue South, Nashville, TN 37202-0801.

This book is printed on recycled, acid-free, elemental-chlorine–free paper.

ISBN 0-687-11109-9

CIP data available from the Library of Congress.

Scripture quotations noted KJV are from the King James Version of the Bible.

Those noted NIV are taken from the Holy Bible: New International Version. Copyright © 1973, 1978, 1984 by the International Bible Society. Used by permission of Zondervan Bible Publishers.

Those noted NRSV are from the New Revised Standard Bible, copyright © 1989 by the Division of Christian Education of the National Council of the Churches of Christ in the United States of America, and are used by permission.

97 98 99 00 01 02 03 04 05 06 — 10 9 8 7 6 5 4 3 2 1

MANUFACTURED IN THE UNITED STATES OF AMERICA

*You show me the path of life.
In your presence there is
fullness of joy;
in your right hand
are pleasures forevermore.*

—Psalm 16:11 NRSV

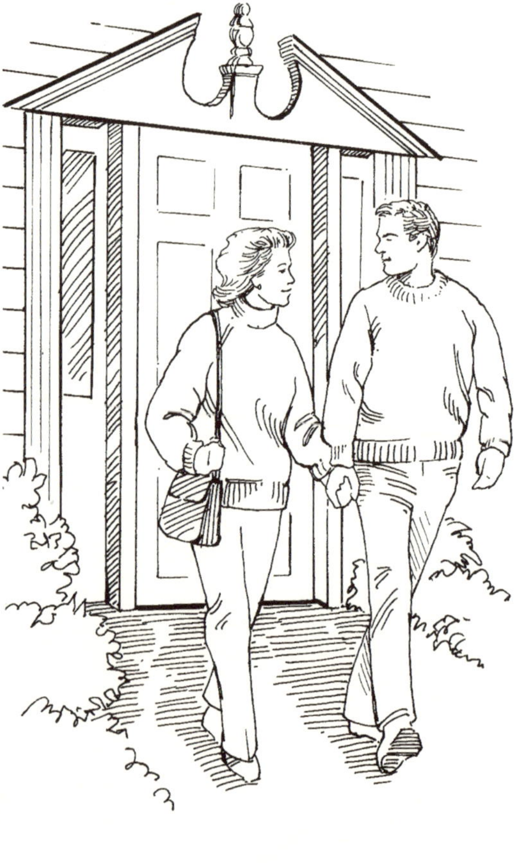

## One

Designate one night a week as date night. Take turns choosing what you will do together.

*Follow the way of love.*

—I Corinthians 14:1 NIV

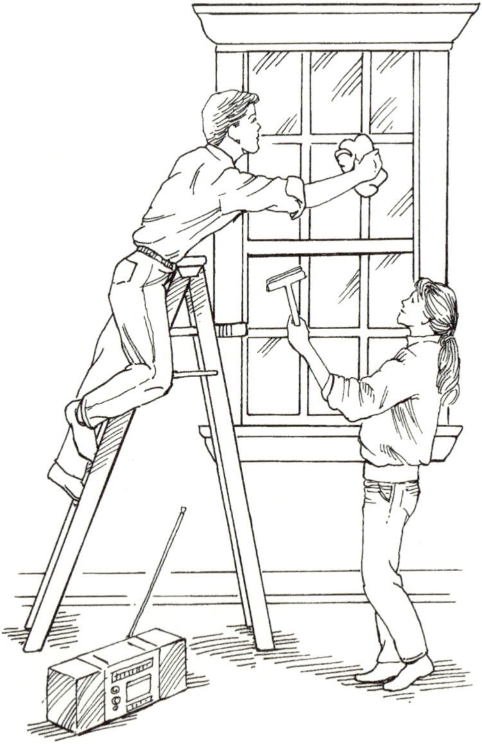

## Two

Clean the house together. Turn on some music and dance and sing while you work.

*All to whom God gives wealth, and possessions, and whom he enables to enjoy them, and to accept their lot and find enjoyment in their toil—this is the gift of God.*

—Ecclesiastes 5:19 NRSV

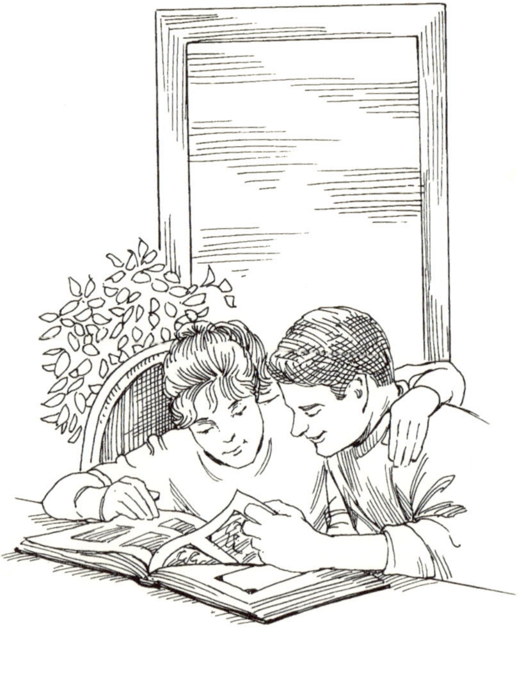

# Three

# Spend an evening looking at your wedding photos.

*"It is not good for man to be alone."*

—Genesis 2:18 NIV

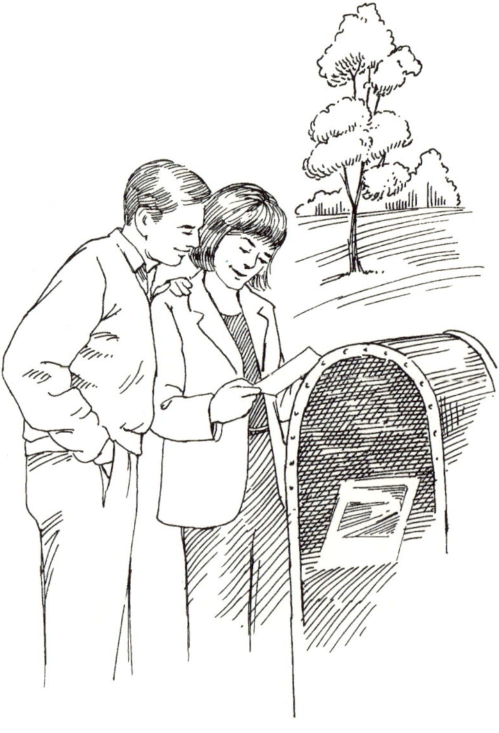

## Four

Wedding ceremonies and the events surrounding them often pass in a blur. Near the time of your anniversary, send a note to your bridesmaids or groomsmen thanking them for their part in your happiness.

*Where your treasure is, there your heart will be also.*

—Matthew 6:21 NIV

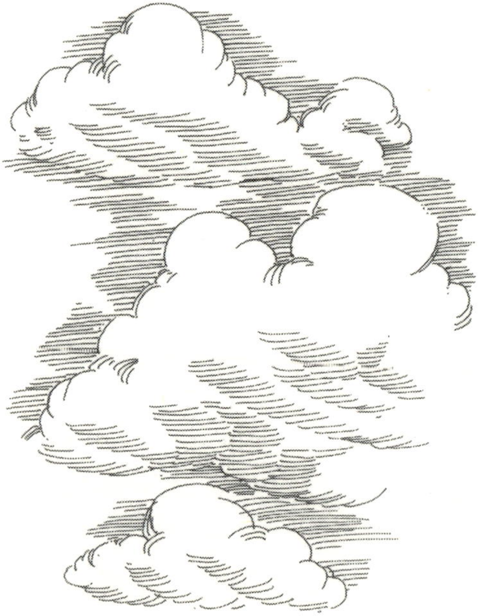

# Five

$\mathscr{S}$pread a blanket in your yard and watch the clouds or count the stars.

This is the day which the LORD hath made;
we will rejoice and be glad in it.

—Psalm 118:24 KJV

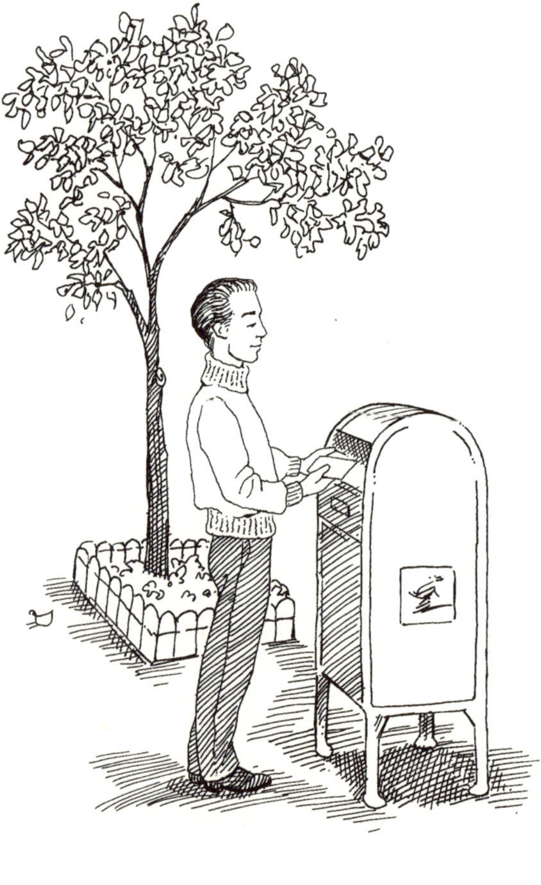

## Six

Write a letter to your spouse's parents telling them how much you love their child.

*He shall be unto thee a restorer of thy life, and a nourisher of thine old age: for thy daughter in law, which loveth thee, which is better to thee than seven sons, hath borne him.*

—Ruth 4:15 KJV

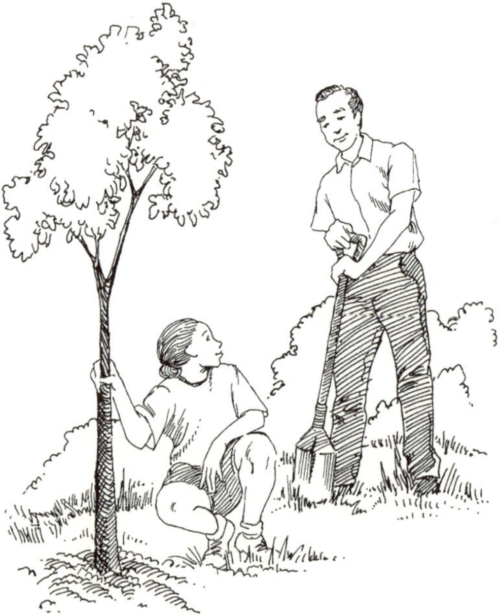

## Seven

Plant a tree on your anniversary. It doesn't have to be in your yard—a school, church, or nursing home would be a delighted recipient.

*I made me gardens and orchards, and I planted trees in them of all kind of fruits.*

—Ecclesiastes 2:5 KJV

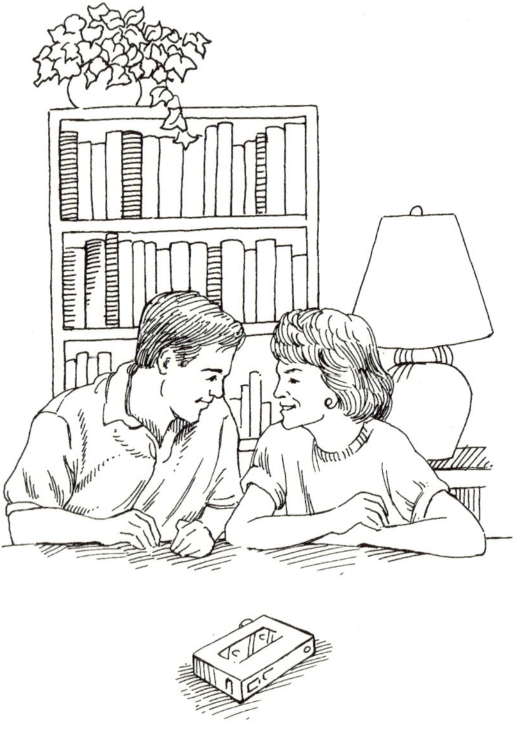

## Eight

*B*uy (or borrow from the library) books on tape. After both of you have finished, spend a date night talking about the book.

*For wisdom will come into your heart,
and knowledge will be
pleasant to your soul.*

—Proverbs 2:10 NRSV

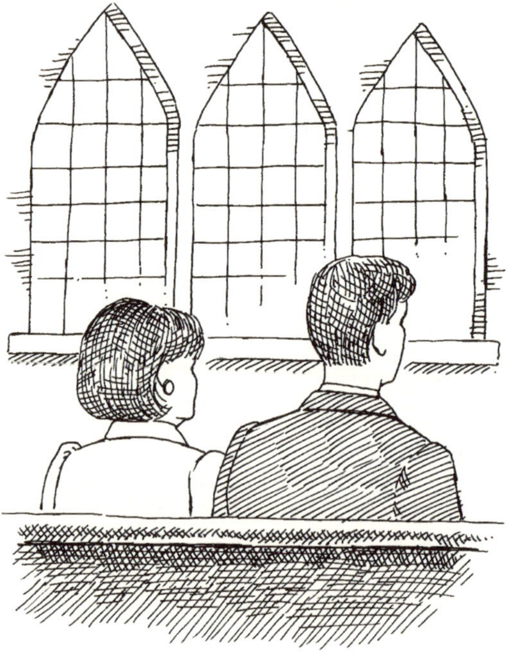

# Nine

Take "time out" from responsibilities at church (choir, nursery, or whatever), every few months so you can sit together at worship.

*Each of you, however, should love his wife as himself, and a wife should respect her husband.*

—Ephesians 5:33 NRSV

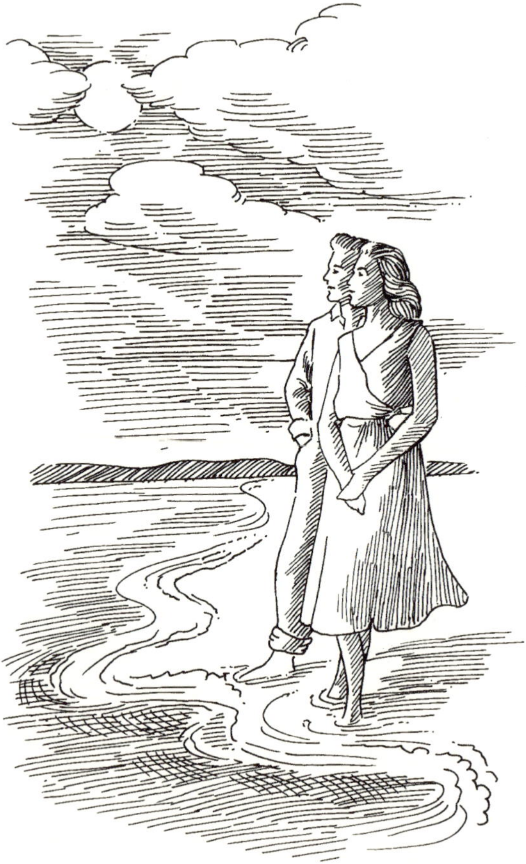

## Ten

Take a moonlight walk together before going to bed. Be sure to hold hands.

When I consider thy heavens, the work of thy fingers, the moon and the stars, which thou hast ordained; what is man, that thou art mindful of him?

—Psalm 8:3-4 KJV

JIM,
DINNER WAS
DELICIOUS!
THANK YOU
FOR COOKING
LAST NIGHT.
LOVE,
ANN

## Eleven

*W*rite a note to your spouse saying how much you appreciate a chore that he or she has done.

*Do everything in love.*

—1 Corinthians 16:14 NIV

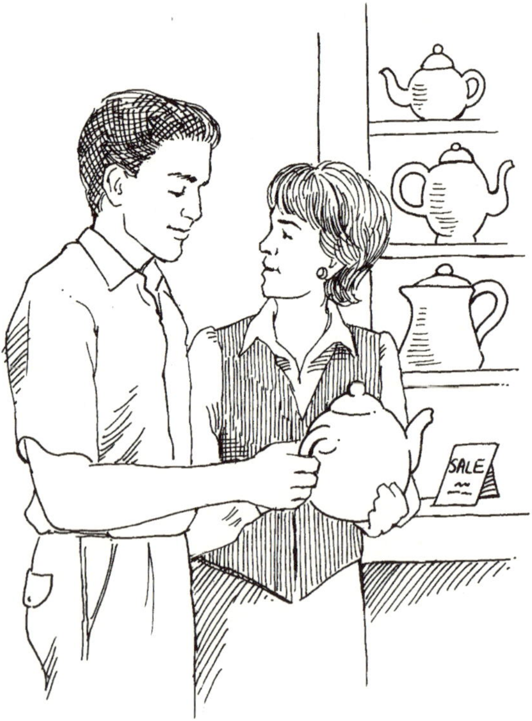
SALE

# Twelve

Start a new collection together. You can have great fun searching out pieces at flea markets and estate sales.

I *gathered me also silver and gold, and the peculiar treasure of kings and of the provinces.*

—Ecclesiastes 2:8 KJV

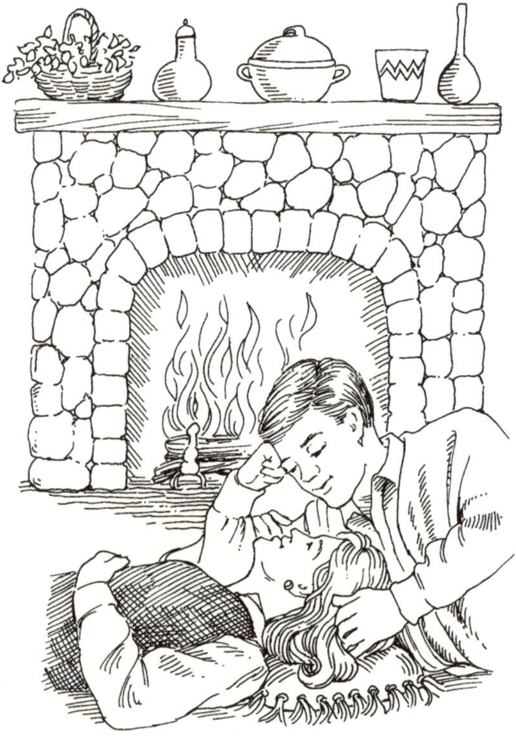

# Thirteen

Buy a cassette tape or compact disc with songs that were popular when you were dating. Play it once a month as background music while you spend time talking and relaxing together.

*Set me as a seal upon your heart.*

—Song of Solomon 8:6 NRSV

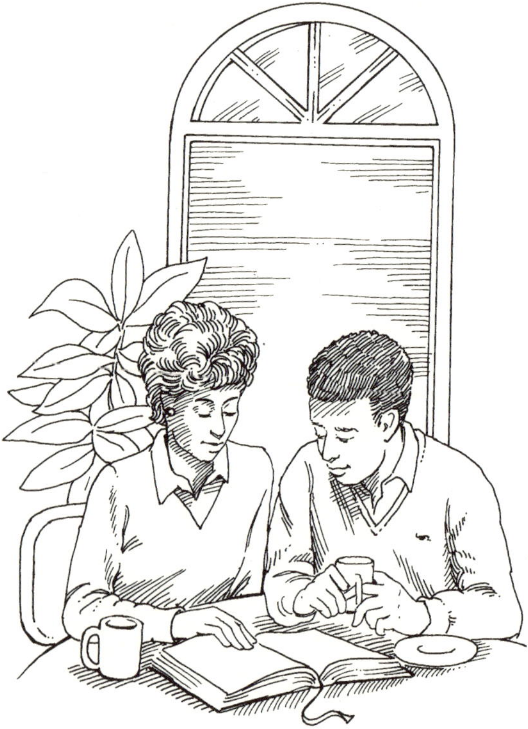

# Fourteen

## Read the Song of Solomon together.

*You have stolen my heart
with one glance of your eyes.*

—Song of Solomon 4:9 NIV

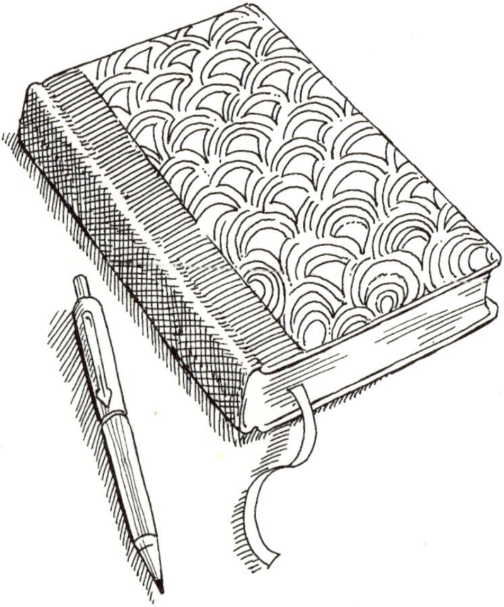

## Fifteen

*K*eep a journal of your life together. Resolve to record at least one happy memory each week.

*This is my prayer, that your love may overflow more and more with knowledge and full insight to determine what is best.*

—Philippians 1:9-10 NRSV

## Sixteen

# Volunteer together at a homeless shelter.

*Every generous act of giving, with every perfect gift, is from above, coming down from the Father of lights, with whom there is no variation or shadow due to change.*

—James 1:17 NRSV

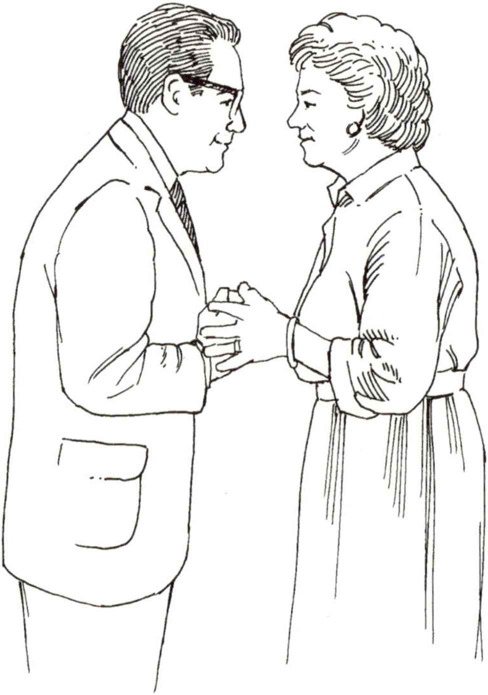

# Seventeen

Reaffirm your marriage vows on your wedding anniversary.

*What . . . God hath joined together, let not man put asunder.*

—Mark 10:9 KJV

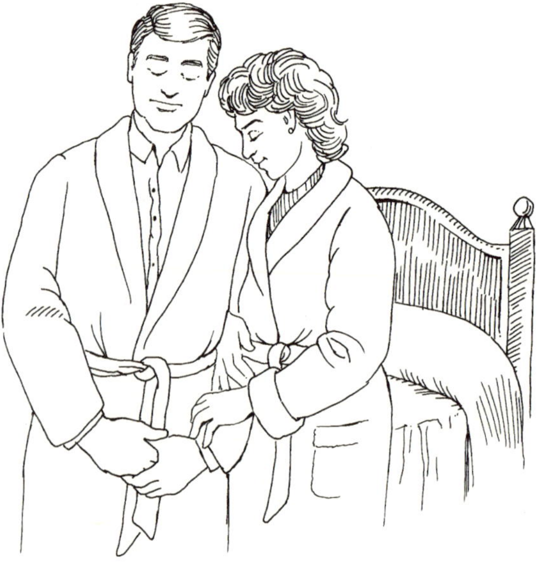

## Eighteen

## Start every day by praying together.

*Whenever you stand praying, forgive, if you have anything against anyone.*

—Mark 11:25 NRSV

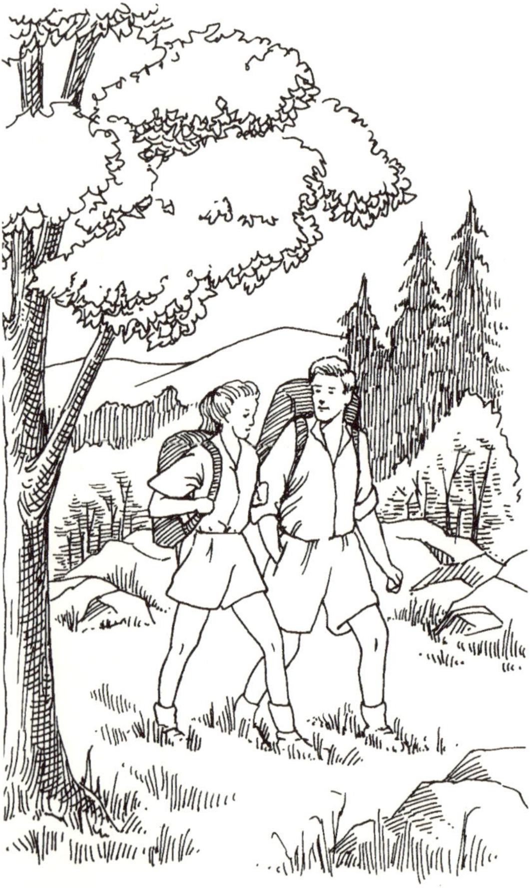

# Nineteen

Find a sport you can enjoy together such as tennis, bowling, or hiking (or learn to be a fan).

A *happy heart makes the face cheerful.*

—Proverbs 15:13 NIV

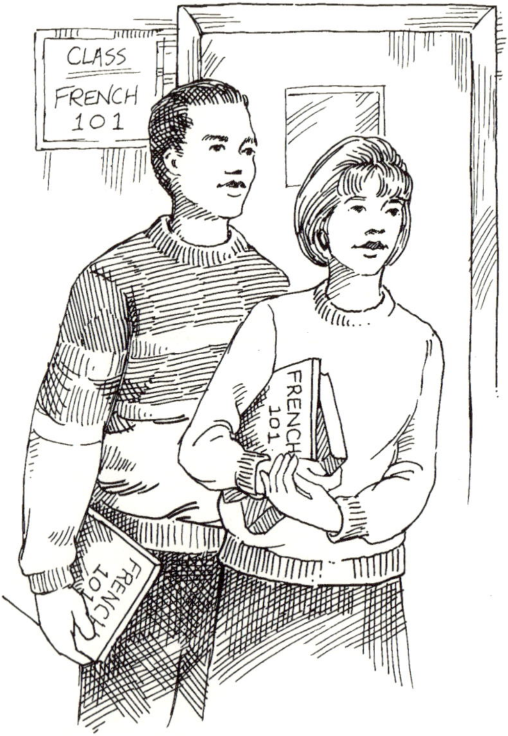
CLASS
FRENCH
101
FRENCH
101
FRENCH
101

## Twenty

Learn a foreign language together. Nearby community colleges offer very inexpensive classes. New friends will be a plus.

*How is it that we hear, each of us, in our own native language?*

—Acts 2:8 NRSV

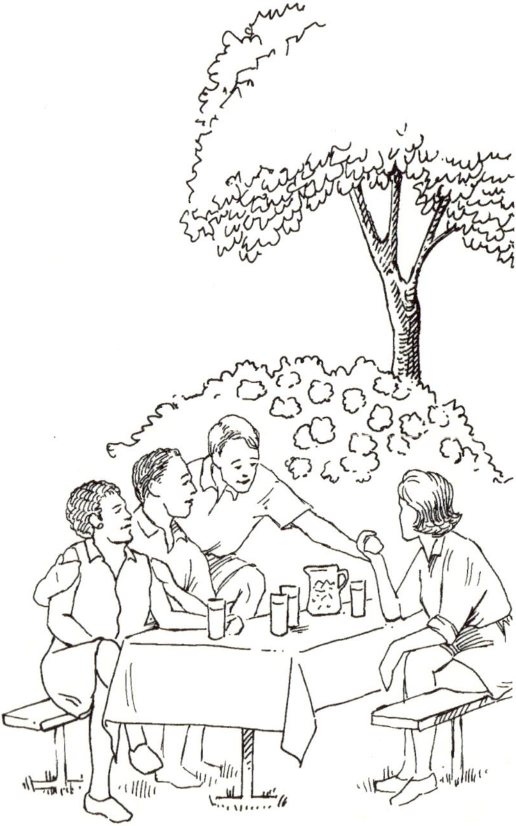

# Twenty-One

Become mentors for an engaged couple. Ask your pastor for ways you can help.

*My purpose is that they may be encouraged in heart and united in love.*

—Colossians 2:2 NIV

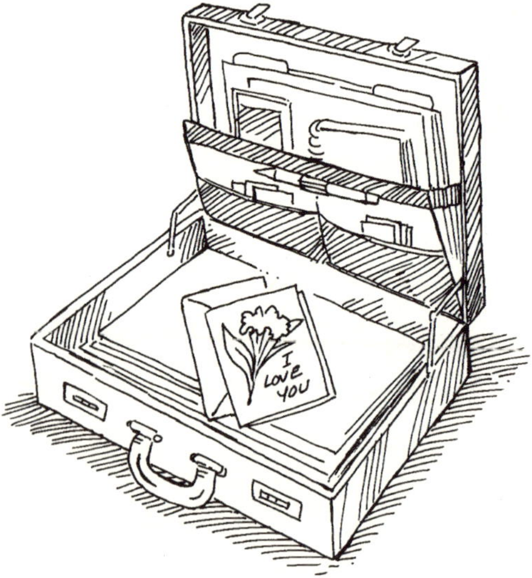
I
LOVE
YOU

## Twenty-two

*T*uck an "I love you" card into a briefcase or lunch sack on a dreary day.

*Encourage one another and build each other up.*

—1 Thessalonians 5:11 NIV

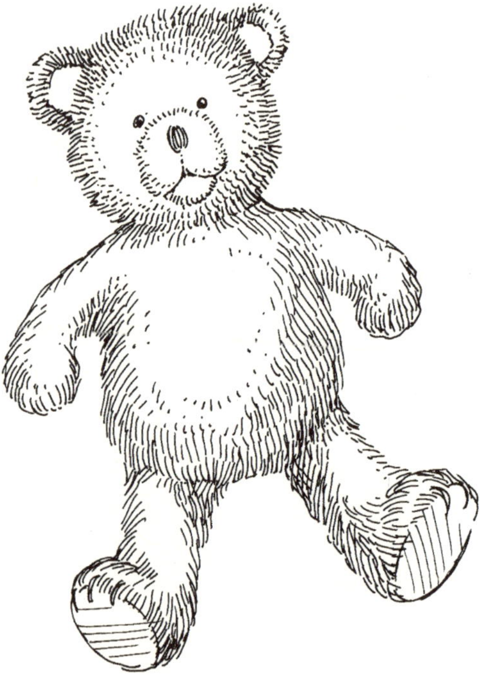

# Twenty-three

*B*uy your spouse a toy he or she always wanted as a child but never got.

*Each of you must give as you have made up your mind, not reluctantly or under compulsion, for God loves a cheerful giver.*

—2 Corinthians 9:7 NRSV

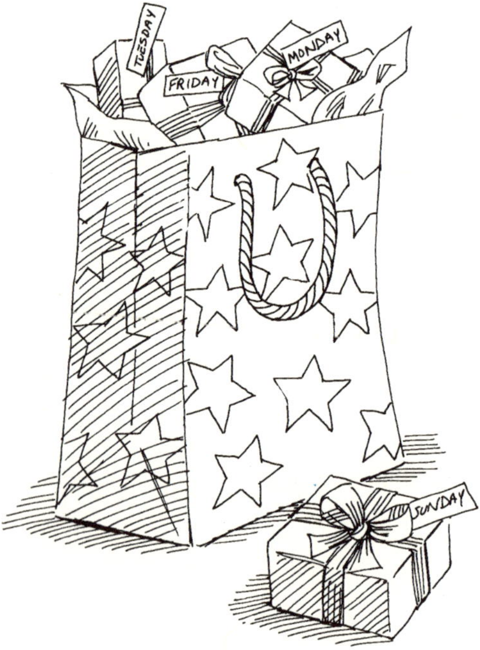
TUESDAY
FRIDAY
MONDAY
SUNDAY

## Twenty-four

Fill a gift bag with seven small presents—one for each day of the week.

*Out of the abundance of the heart
the mouth speaketh.*

—Matthew 12:34 KJV

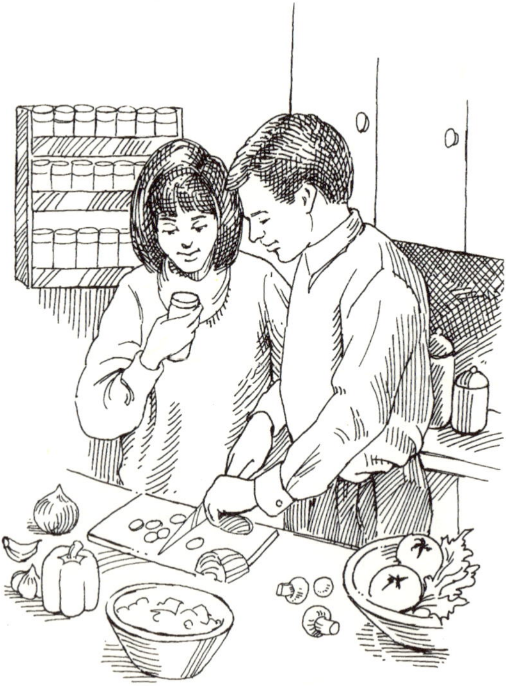

# Twenty-five

## Invent a recipe together. Make it once a month.

*Better a meal of vegetables where there is love than a fattened calf with hatred.*

—Proverbs 15:17 NIV

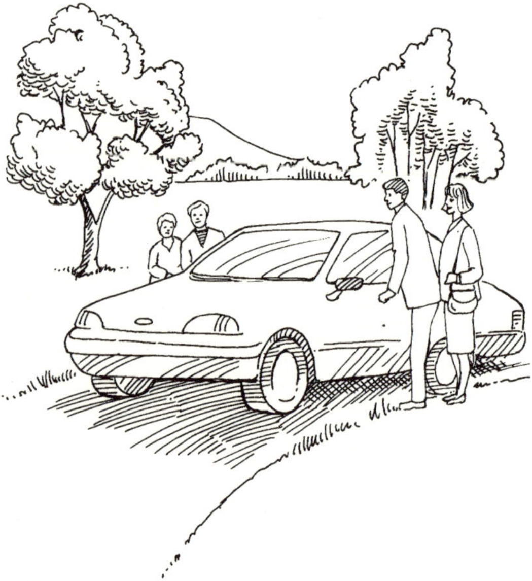

## Twenty-six

Invite each set of parents to go on a date with you (separately!).

*Agree with one another, live in peace; and the God of love and peace will be with you.*

—2 Corinthians 13:11 NRSV

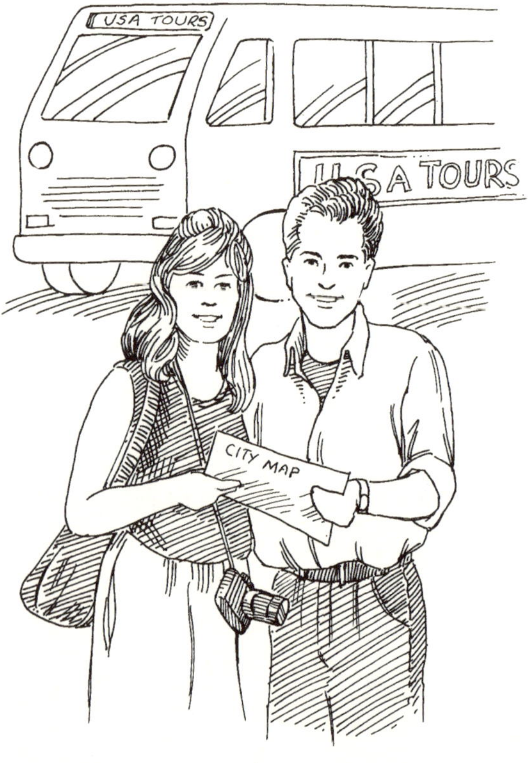
USA TOURS
USA TOURS
CITY MAP

## Twenty-seven

Become tourists for a day in your own city. Visit an attraction neither of you has seen before.

*He looked for a city which hath foundations, whose builder and maker is God.*

—Hebrews 11:10 KJV

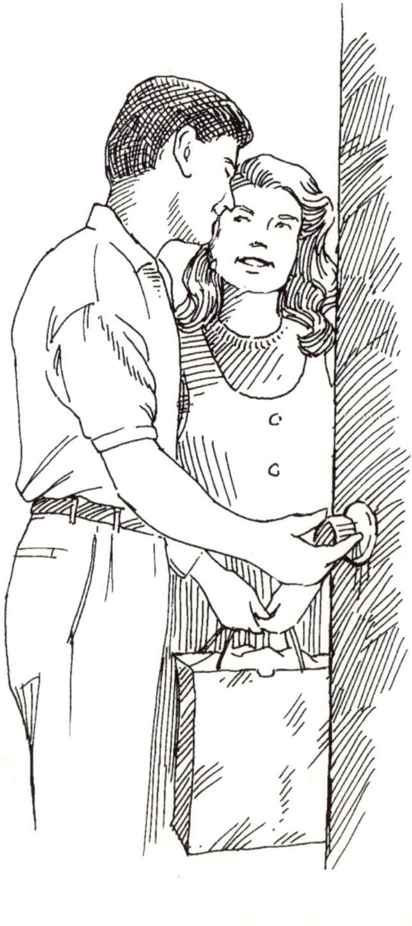

# Twenty-eight

## Relive your first date.

*Above all else, guard your heart,
for it is the wellspring of life.*

—Proverbs 4:23 NIV

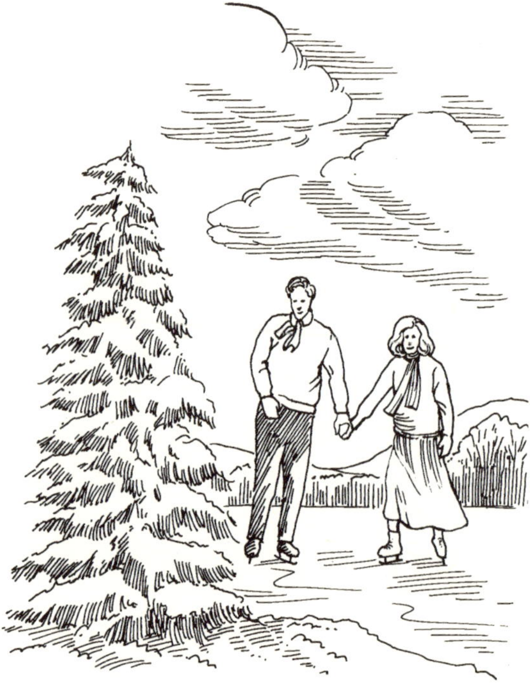

## Twenty-nine

Start new traditions of your very own for holidays, weekends, or other special days.

*Commemorate this day . . .*

—Exodus 13:3 NIV

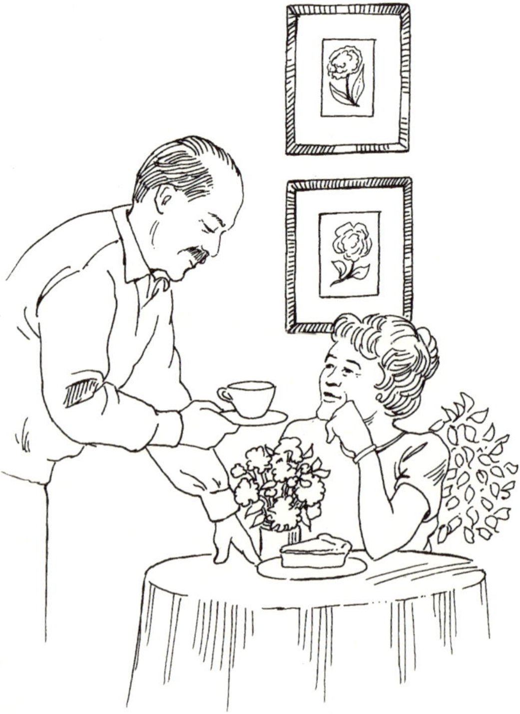

# Thirty

Adopt an elderly couple. Ask them their secrets of a happy marriage.

*Now abideth faith, hope, charity, these three; but the greatest of these is charity.*

—1 Corinthians 13:13 KJV